brave little sternums: poems from Rojava

Matt Broomfield

First published 8th July 2022 by Fly on the Wall Press
Published in the UK by
Fly on the Wall Press
56 High Lea Rd
New Mills
Derbyshire
SK22 3DP

www.flyonthewallpress.co.uk
ISBN: 978-1-913211-81-3
EBOOK: 978-1-913211-95-0
Copyright Matt Broomfield © 2022

The right of Matt Broomfield to be identified as the author of this work has been asserted in accordance with the Copyright, Designs and Patents Act 1988.

Typesetting by Isabelle Kenyon. Cover illustration by Lisa Lorenz. All photography credited with thanks to the Rojava Information Centre.

All rights reserved. No part of this publication may be reproduced, stored in or introduced into a retrieval system, or transmitted in any form, or by any means (electronic, mechanical, photocopying, recording or otherwise) without prior written permissions of the publisher. Any person who does any unauthorised act in relation to this publication may be liable for criminal prosecution and civil claims for damages.

This is a work of fiction. Names, characters, business, events and incidents are the products of the author's imagination. Any resemblance to actual persons, living or dead, or actual events is purely coincidental.

A CIP Catalogue record for this book is available from the British Library.

For Mehmet Aksoy (Firaz Dag), and all those writers, journalists and artists who have given their lives in the pursuit of truth in Kurdistan.

Praise for *brave little sternums*

"In these poems there is a human cry that is deeper than war or friendship alone. Broomfield has a precise pen, delicate emotions, and a deep love of people. He refuses to accept war, the occupation of nature, looting or destruction. As one enters into these poems, one sees a search for what is precious, the growth of nations, a desire for happiness, peace, equality and a world for everyone. These poems were written during Broomfield's time in our country, where he decorated each moment with golden words. Each poem expresses a different moment in the revolution, each word returns to comradeship, and this book will be a gift to history. Broomfield's pen is precious. His feelings even more so."
- Nergiz Ismail, poet from Rojava

"Like the Rojavan revolution he describes, Broomfield's poems are alive and writhing, unsparing in self-analysis and honest about the complex realities of translating theory into governance. It's clear that these poems were written on the ground, in community and conversation, and their reflection of that experience has given this reader a richer, more human understanding than any academic theorizing or factual reportage. 'brave little sternums' is not just literature about Rojava, it's an essential contribution to the literature of Rojava, equally conversant with contemporary English and Kurmanji-language poetry."
- David Shook, poet and Kurdish translator

"Hard words about a terrible injustice: the continued oppression of the people of Rojava."
- Attila the Stockbroker, poet

"A series of lenses into a bruised world—where the land itself is sometimes fertilized with the teeth of the dead. The voice here is raw and unvarnished, with a shot of adrenaline burning on the tongue. You'll find that beneath the cynic's hard gaze is a deep and abiding love, one that arrives from the interior of history, one that speaks passionately about fundamental issues of justice and human dignity in verses so restless and disturbed the page can barely contain them."
- Brian Turner, author of Here, Bullet

Author's note:

Readers who are not familiar with recent developments in Syria, Kurdistan and the Middle East may find useful the following brief summary of events in the region. Additionally, a glossary explaining terms, locations and references that may be unfamiliar follows the collection, along with a number of textual notes.

I believe, with Brecht, that introducing the reader to some specifics of a story (or poem) ahead of time will not limit their understanding to a particular interpretation; on the contrary, it will enable them to see and understand the material conditions which gave rise to a particular story, and thus to understand both these particularities, and how the content might be relevant to their own place and time.

As Brecht says: "Only the lessons of reality can teach us to transform reality."

This is a partisan history. In other words, it is a story.

In brief: the Kurds, numbering up to forty million, are among the most numerous peoples in the world not to have a nation-state of their own. As a result of Western colonial intervention, the historic region of Kurdistan was divided among four modern states: Turkey (occupying Bakur, or Northern Kurdistan); Iraq (occupying Bashur, or Southern Kurdistan); Iran (occupying Rojhilat, or Eastern Kurdistan); and Syria (occupying Rojava, or

Western Kurdistan). Successive regimes in all four states have conducted policies of genocide, warfare, cultural, political and linguistic extermination against the Kurdish people, resulting in centuries of conflict and armed resistance.

The Kurdish freedom movement began its contemporary existence as a Marxist-Leninist guerilla force fighting against the Turkish government to establish an independent, socialist Kurdistan. Following an internal political struggle led by female members, the Kurdistan Workers' Party (PKK) became known for the special prominence it placed on the role of women in liberating society. A further, significant change in political paradigm followed the 1999 capture and imprisonment of Kurdish figurehead and PKK founder Abdullah Öcalan.

While in prison, Öcalan published writings advocating for a new political approach he terms 'democratic confederalism'. He both draws on and critiques Marxist-Leninist and anarchist thought, as well as actually-existing communist projects, national liberation struggles, social democracy and the feminist movement. He argues that the repressive nation-state and patriarchal repression of women must both be overcome before any true democracy or socialism can be achieved. As such, the PKK—and its associated parties across Kurdistan—stopped fighting for a Kurdish state *per se*. Instead, they now seek to establish a decentralised, egalitarian, community-based system in Kurdistan and across the Middle East.

This ideology was put into practice in and around the Turkish state, and in other areas of Kurdistan, but found by far its fullest expression following the wave of anti-authoritarian protests known as the 'Arab Spring' and the outbreak of the Syrian revolution. As dictator Bashar al-Assad's forces withdrew from Kurdish regions of Syria to repress pro-democracy uprisings elsewhere in Syria, they likely thought they were abandoning Rojava to be over-run by the Islamist militias already ascendant in the Syrian opposition.

But Rojava did not fall. Instead, on the basis of decades of clandestine organising by Kurdish *hevals* (comrades), the region was able to rapidly establish democratic self-governance. To do so, the region first had to survive successive, overlapping wars and battles against ISIS, the Turkish Armed Forces, and Islamist militias including al-Qaeda offshoot the al-Nusra Front, as well as the Assad regime itself.

As ISIS swept through the region, it was Rojava's well-known YPG and YPJ armed forces who were the first to put up effective resistance. By handing ISIS their first major defeat at the siege of Kobane in 2014, the region gained worldwide support—and an unlikely alignment with the US-led International Coalition to Defeat ISIS. The Kurdish movement was now working alongside NATO's largest army (the USA) on the one hand, while facing brutal attacks from NATO's second-largest army (Turkey) on the other—the latter occurring with political support, technology and clandestine intelligence from the USA and its allies in Europe.

A string of victories against ISIS enabled the 'Rojava revolution' to spread beyond Kurdish areas, establishing a remarkable system of direct-democratic governance across a region home to some four million people, based on principles of devolved democracy and women's autonomy. Öcalan's ideology also prioritizes self-determination, co-existence and religious and ethnic plurality, on the basis of political self-organisation among the region's diverse communities. To mark its expansion, the region adopted a new, official name—North and East Syria (NES). Kurds no longer make up the majority of the population of NES—millions of Arabs, plus Yezidis and Syriac, Assyrian and Armenian Christians, along with other minorities, participate in the revolution today. Even Raqqa, the one-time capital of the ISIS caliphate, is now a proud bastion of the women's revolution.

But though ISIS has been eradicated as a territorial entity, NES has faced two successive and devastating Turkish invasions and occupations. Turkey attacked the regions of Afrin in 2018 and Sere Kaniye and Tel Abyad in 2019. The former invasion was green-lit by Russian President Vladimir Putin, the latter by then-US President Donald Trump. Trump's involvement briefly drew the world's attention to NES, as US troops partially withdrew from the region.

Each invasion resulted in the death of hundreds and the displacement of hundreds of thousands of civilians, most of them Kurds and other minorities, as Turkey conducts a policy of forcible ethnic cleansing in regions it now occupies. Following a 'ceasefire' agreement, the border region is de facto divided between Turkish and NES control, in what is officially a new 'safe zone' patrolled by US and Russian forces, but where conflict remains a daily reality.

In the Turkish-occupied regions—which, while they were still part of NES, enjoyed Syria's highest standards of democracy, humanitarian conditions, and rule of law—rape, torture, execution, forced disappearance and other atrocities committed by Turkey and its proxies are commonplace. Turkey continues to violate the nominal ceasefire, with shelling and drone strikes. NES also faces a partial economic embargo, total lack of international recognition, and repeated attempts on behalf of its nominal partners in the region and the West to undermine, destabilize or strangle the revolution. At the same time, practical and ideological compromises have been made as the revolution has spread from Kurdish heartlands to cover a huge swathe of territory and population, including many religious and conservative regions where principles of democracy and gender liberation clash with traditional values.

Against all odds, though, the Rojava revolution survives to this day. This is thanks to thousands of locals who sacrificed their lives in defence of the region. All of these individuals are remembered and honoured by people across NES as the *shehids* (martyrs) who made the revolution possible.

Dozens of international volunteers also gave their lives to defend NES and the principles it stands for. Other 'internationalist' volunteers, such as myself, have travelled to the region to work in solidarity with the revolution in a civilian capacity—some as women's organisers, ecological experts, medical staff or engineers, all with the aim of learning from the unique political programme in the region. I arrived in NES shortly after Afrin fell to Turkey in March 2018, and remained there until the end of 2020—the 2019 war against Turkey forms the third section of the poems collected below. Almost all the poems in the collection were written in NES.

As a professional writer and journalist, my role was to help to co-found the Rojava Information Centre, the region's top independent news and research source. In this capacity, I was fortunate to risk far less than many other local and foreign volunteers—and to see the revolution from many sides, in many places, alongside many people. It was the most humbling, challenging and moving experience of my life. So much primary-coloured propaganda and grey criticism has been written about Rojava, totally missing the real energy of the place. The revolution is living, ugly, beautiful, writhing, self-contradictory, hopelessly compromised—and utterly worth fighting for.

Berxwedan jiyan e! Resistance is life!

Matt Broomfield, February 2022

Contents:

I – *The crime of sitting very still*

for the hunger strikers, Amed prison	15
X was having sleepovers; Y used to sleep out; who's the real dope boy?	17
road repair works continue in Tirbespi	19
kisses rough through the ski mask but	21
civilian civilian civilian	23
for Sakine Cansiz	26
crowd simulation	28
ghazal: 80km from Shengal city	35

II – *Temporary Northern Syria Buffer Zone*

safe zone	41
apo apo we were talking about apo	43
new rules	45
Can Yoldashim	47
to kill the man inside	48
WhatsApp is the weapon	51
apobaterion	53
in fieri	55
lifestyle treacherous	57
'shame is a revolutionary virtue'	60
internationalism	61
to not self-educate is to betray	62
situations	64
such flags	66

Temporary Northern Syria Buffer Zone,
2019-2019   68
Qamishlo   70

III – Operation Peace Spring

balance sheet   81
for our enemies   83
ISIS withdraw from their last urban stronghold...   85
absence of evidence   88
for Hevrin Khalef   90
when elephants dance   92
for M., in England   94
to the retreating convoy   96
Peace Spring   97

IV – Marvellous as fancy parakeets

ceasefire   101
Peace Spring ii   103
pathogen unknown   105
for Anna Campbell (Helin Qerechox)   108
Korinthos pre-removal detention centre   110
reduction   111
prison sestina iv   113
david wojnarowicz drinks a tea in kobane   116
through the bars   118
mucky pups   120
these are the years   121

I – The crime of sitting very still

for the hunger strikers, Amed prison

our enemies are mad because we have discovered
the crime of sitting very still

mothers mostly commit it, in the privacy
of the martyred parts of themselves
to remain like a stone or a lump in the breast:
wicked are the ways of women

scarcely off four legs, we huddle
in the clag of kindled embers
while bone beats on bone in the fastness above
and you think you have the rhythm to horrify us?

please

we were calm as you took one in ten of us
we were calm as we nine were taken too
in those days we learned the crime
of looking very hard at what we saw

you built prisons for lives to race past in
there, we learned how to wait out the years
how to throw stones without swinging the arm
how to let go at just the right time

this is not to say
those pretty darlings in Diyarbakir were our last
this is not to say
we will not govend-movend all over your graves
this is not to say
we will not take up the gun
with the stillness that comes
once every other move has been made

tak tak tak
sometimes, it's just like that

these days, we say *up the RA* and the RA keep rising
these days, it doesn't matter if we lose
a long hot summer is nothing to be mad in
try thirty-eight years on the boil

didn't you ever want to be part of a movement
much slower than yourself?

X was having sleepovers; Y used to sleep out;
who's the real dope boy?

i read: *chief keef is chief of nothing*
guess that means he's chief of something
white boys getting hard-ons
on suburban afternoons

form a gun with crooked fingers
in the pocket of my coat
cops never stop me anyway
palm sweat slick on the trigger finger anyway

thought gunplay made you heavy
all it does is make me thirsty
never was any good
at shooting games anyway

white boys on knifepoint
mom's spaghetti
child soldiers in minefields
mom's spaghetti

had a dream about war
but i never saw war
so i dreamed *star wars: the phantom menace*
it was war but the phantom menace

the barrel bombs fell anyway
the sucking wounds sucked anyway
and i stayed shook
like a bitch boy at gunpoint

but then i never was at gunpoint
was i?
still mumbling *still not loving police*
still shook like an aspen leaf

road repair works continue in Tirbespi

we have laughed at the evening news
repeating itself each day

same reports on potholes in the undeveloped road
same shaming of the same old crimes

hard to find anything to report on
among nested states of exception

hard to say anything apart from
things have continued in this way

hard to remember before
there was remembering

when boys since deceased dropped fireworks
in the pockets of greatcoated police

when girls lifted girls on shoulders
to spray Y P J on out-of-reach walls

hard to speak of what should be spoken of
to know what the censors allow

a flower in place of the martyr photo
means the martyr was underage when she died

well-maintained roads lead to the peoples' hearts
so our comrades say

Ape Yusif, who remembers the French Mandate,
tells me: *ah, but the roads were smooth*

the roads are smoother today than they were before
before before, they were smoother still

still, all things considered,
this may be counted a miracle

kisses rough through the ski mask but

if the boy doesn't want me to see his face
the boy doesn't want me to see his face
anyway, we know one another
in spite of our fears and the kevlar sheath

i make him moan in the right way
he consents to relocate me to the coast
each wrong turn a mock execution
still, it proves possible to sleep

subway switching trainers like
we're not cuffed since the first trimester
crossing biometric borders
like it's nothing. like a dance

dead drops in Balkan squats
no way, not here: yet here we are
snorting state-backed courage
from spent passports in airport loos

all these sim cards switched and swallowed
checkpoints sashayed through
all this time we thought we were nervous
we weren't nearly nervous enough

wicked to move so careless, maybe
how else should i continue to care?
bugged out crossing borders
still, i can cross them. so i cross

civilian civilian civilian

always talking about
sourdough, tort law
breast work, trench shit

never heard that *astaghfirullah*
in the manufactory, that shangri-la
chasing that cancer

chasing that bug shit
everything always inadvisable
holding the coldest

six years of octobers
that fellow shooter who ad-libs
the name of his brother

the civil service shadowed
the skulls rubberised, the four o'clock
car crash endless, inevitable

u wish u had crystals
to split gems
with good sisters

to be brave
or at least
to be high

for Sakine Cansiz

she wouldn't shut up about what must not be shut up about.
honour her by shutting up for good. Go-Pro star
claiming cannibal. sequinned headscarf money-shot.
don't you know we're six shepherds all at once?

when bodies drip from back-hoes no wonder vloggers
get to salivating, specifying *rainy season* though it's winter
here also, magnifying ritual slits in pectoral muscles
ten times with no mention of the Medya Defence Zones

where meadows swallow drones and the people endure.
milkmaid with the hand-grenade, she needs no micro-finance. honour her by hiding combatant fishwives in wardrobes.
commit crimes that leave the Palme d'Or jury displeased.

where were you when padlocks got blown off cultural centres?
where were you when letters were erased from names?
where were you when real gunmen crossed over your borders?
when smuggled paint touched flesh and went up beautiful?

he who douses is the traitor, she who comforts
is the soldier, she who petrol-bombs also
they who have no rest put Kurdistan on women's shoulders
before they spoke a word they'd broken one law

Sakine Cansiz was a leading female figurehead of the Kurdish freedom movement, who spent years in jail in Turkey, facing torture and other abuses. She and two other female Kurdish activists were shot dead in a Kurdish Cultural Centre in Paris in 2013, by a gunman linked to the Turkish-controlled Grey Wolves fascist paramilitary group.

crowd simulation

"I guess Trump wasn't 'Putin's puppet' after all, he was just another deep state/Neo-Con puppet" / "There isn't a 'Syrian war', certainly not 'civil war', there is multi-national imperialist war ON Syria, led by the US-NATO + puppet States"/ "If Trump thinks dropping bombs is the Mother of All Distractions, this could become more frequent. Do not lose focus on Trump-Russia ties…"

- *responses by three Western commentators to US President Donald Trump targeting the Assad government's Shayrat Airbase with cruise missiles in April 2017, following the Khan Sheikoun chemical weapons attack.*

$$I_a = \begin{cases} c & \text{if } p_a \in A \\ 0 & \text{if } p_a \notin A \end{cases}$$ - *formula used to model the impact of environmental stressors on an individual forming part of a crowd in a high-stress situation.*

Syria does not exist. *the behaviour of crowds in high-stress situations can be modelled using General Adaptation Syndrome (GAS) theory,* and so it was more cost-effective to fake the whole affair.

Syria does not exist. we hacked off the protective visors from the helmets we used to fake the moon landing and gave them to our operatives, all of them actors, even the children writhing among freshly-sloughed skin like the lizards which, in truth, control nothing: not the oil reserves, nor the new but increasingly passé world order, nor the awful spasming of their limbs. *agent behaviour is affected by various environmental stressors categorized into four prototypes: time pressure, area pressure, positional stressors, and interpersonal stressors.*

Syria does not exist. we raised each agent alone from birth, plugged into perfect simulations of the digital sandbox called Sham, running scripts to perfectly track and replicate each stochastic speck of silt in the life-giving Euphrates. to accurately model the crisis of authoritarian nationalism in the Arab world it was necessary to first plot the antediluvian breaking of bread and obsidian flints; the cuneiform kingdoms each raised on the stumps of the last; the trade in textiles and amphoras of oil down through booming Ugarit across the breakers to the wild world beyond, over-run by the Hittites and the Mittanis and the Sea People and Assyrians and Suteans and Arameans and Phoenicians and Neo-Assyrians and Scythians and Babylonians and Macedonians and Seleucidans and Judean Hasmoneans and the fucking MENA analysts. each of these was generated by the very latest in CIA stress-based system technology, and/or massaged into life by skilled Russian operatives.

to simulate an environment is easy. *various models have been proposed to define how the body reacts to stressors*, and ours necessitates the most careful calibration of all the parameters of what you now call 'Syria', the Damascene spring-time and the jasmine flowering, the jet skis breaking surf off the Latakian coast, every arcade and each arabesque of the Masjid al-Umayyad, the tooled leather and the copper-work, the clatter of backgammon, the

phones buzzing with PUBG, the white light streaming through the high glass windows.

the beginning is game theory and the rest soon follows, taking on its own life, exceeding the coders' wildest dreams. strange forms emerging at random from the neolithic code in its inchoate dawn. Hafez al-Assad raising mosques from the smoke of slaughter. the ophthalmologist crowned butcher. *when the threat or stressor is identified or realized, the body enters the first stage of the GAS model: alarm.* if a bloodless coup should turn bloody, no matter. the coder's steady hand will run the simulation back, recalibrate the parameters, and press play once again. *during the alarm phase, the body can endure changes such as hypovolemia, hypoosmolality, hyponatremia, hypochloremia and hypoglycemia. this is the stressor effect.*

we did not bomb them in 1925. we did not bomb them in '26. we did not bomb them in '45. the programme ran so perfectly we almost forgot the bombs did not exist, so elegantly rendered were the broken-framed infants, the eyes guttering out like wax. we did not bomb them in '67. we did not bomb them in '73. *the intensity of the stressor increases as an agent approaches the source of the stress. an example would be a fire or a dynamic object, such as an assailant.* all these bloodless bloodbaths and all these non-events crackling and fizzing around the brainless brains we tended to in vats, the childhoods where no children ran through the high-rises of Aleppo or the tumbling olive groves of Jabal al-Zawiya, the unsanctioned oil fields where the derricks did not swing like the batons which hung dormant round the motionless souqs and silent quads where no students laughed and no doctors strained throats with slogans behind surgical masks and no nurses named the sacred dead. our servers strained and glowed bright red and our crisis actors started the decades-long rumble of pre-rehearsed screams.

we ran the numbers and the time was right. marionettes suspended on strings of binary code swung into action, each believing they moved of their own volition, each garrotting the next with each twitch of their arms. small arms at first, catapults, molotovs: gun-cotton packed in the throat of a terracotta pipe: this was an incremental programme, cunningly devised. we did not arm them in 1982 and we did not arm them in 2011—I mean, we really let them be slaughtered like sheep, boiled in oil in the sewers of Hama, blasted to shreds in the free streets of Homs. really, they almost seemed real.

interpersonal stressors are stressors as a result of crowding by nearby agents. as crowds swell in size, the computing power required to simulate them increases exponentially. the dynamics of rage are not easily captured through abstracted algorithm, since each agent must appear to act autonomously, and such specificities of suffering do not come cheap. in the long run, we determined, it would be more cost-efficient to create what we needed through analogue means. we lashed them to life with lengths of hosepipe and spread them over the waterless earth. we sealed the whole land in a black box and left it to decay in the dark. ghost detainees, extraordinarily rendered, with doses of 10 mA A/C current.

the second GAS stage is: resistance.

this was the bug in the heart of the machine. the grain of silt swept up by an unprogrammed wind, scouring through the servers, lodging in a diode which flipped over in the dark. the mother of all fatherless sons. we hardly feel we are to blame.

the probability model ran over and over and the same scenes recurred. dizzying now, the hacksaws zithering through flesh, the barrel-bombs obscuring the light of the sun, the graves overflowing with the dust of bones, the artificial lives indistinguishable from the real, howling, over-running all our fine algorithms. though we pulled the plug they kept on coming, and whether real or not they died just the same, crawling up the sheer sides of the black box, tumbling into the light.

division and multiplication and division and multiplication and the result was not zero. not quite. *artificial 'ants' (i.e. simulation agents) locate optimal solutions by moving through a parameter space representing all possible solutions.* false flags proliferated till the sky darkened and they beat over each imagined city, Deir-ez-Zor where the youths once swallow-dived from the bridge now sunk below the sucking mire, Palmyra the scarcely inhabited, Bosra the broken-stoned. strange sights drift across our screens.

ghosts in the system. AWOL sprites. all closed systems tend to popular uprising. false binaries ensue: bugs/ghosts. actors/human shields. bad guys/worse. moderate rebels/fanatic observers.

the name 'boid' corresponds to a shortened version of 'bird-oid object', which refers to a bird-like object, which refers to fifty-nine bright silver cruise missiles sinking sub-stratospheric through the sky, devoid of fraud or mystery. this was *real*, this was *right*, sundering the fabric of the simulation to expose the shadow state below, shadow fields, shadow towns, shadow olive groves and souqs, the shadow children still turned inside-out and frothing blood but fading now, light gleaming from the beaks of the TLAMs, exposing each tiny skull as a mask.

real skulls may also have been split by these real bombs, of course: but realistically some collateral must be expected. we are fighting a war, after all.

the shadowed sun is a black pill. take it and look again. consider the uncertain vectors of simulated crowds, the tell-tale recurrence of scenes. consider the backgammon board of the mortar-blasted slums, where soviet stooges and imperial plants keep no tally of the uncountable dead. consider the blank firing ground of the desert earth, the unreal cities not trampled, the olive groves not drenched in immaterial blood.

close your eyes, sheeple. there is nothing left to see here.

The three quotes at the start of the piece come from one alt-right, one Marxist-Leninist, and one neo-liberal commentator. They are united in treating Syria as nothing but a staging ground for Western political concerns.

ghazal: 80km from Shengal city

not knowing your name, i call you *heval*
by that name i know you, *heval*

the rebels announce they shot down a plane
it was a drone, *heval*

militiamen muster, theirs, ours
mostly theirs, *heval*

coffins are carried down the Tel Kocher road
no matter how heavy, *heval*

mothers will wail and reach for the coffin
no matter how empty, *heval*

copters crawl through the vast overhead
most likely the Yanks, *heval*

they fly Pizza Hut pizza into their bases
so Telegram claims, *heval*

Coca-Cola is a symbol of capitalist creep
we drink Pepsi instead, *heval*

people go to the communes for benzene and bread
not for critical theory, *heval*

Shahin was *shehid* on the Deir-ez-Zor front
he came here from France, *heval*

on that same day three Kurds were *shehid*
they were already here, *heval*

seventeen Kurds drowned in the Aegean Sea
they tried to be free, *heval*

Hamid takes selfies with Mazdas in Athens
he tries to be free, *heval*

graffiti in Qamishlo says: *I will not go*
as though there was a choice, *heval*

the UN says: *they make use of suicide bombings*
none wanted to die, *heval*

not all Kurdish women are fearsome guerrillas
some of them are, *heval*

the BBC says: *these women want to be free*
they already are, *heval*

ninety per cent of Kobane fell to the enemy
it did not fall, *heval*

without a choice, they continued to fight
as though there was a choice, *heval*

we have come so far and no further
we have come so far, *heval*

II – Temporary Northern Syria Buffer Zone

safe zone

good god how you stank of benzene and corn oil
the first time i smelled you aflame

living light in the safe zone on MSG sachets
beans and the biweekly egg

music of the spheres quick-step with the squeegee
here, the havens of peace for the wild

here, the pottery shards scrape the fat from the burner
all we wanted was to be left alone

games of the bad boys rushed into and blundered
my nom de guerre bleached into your chest

night walks without small arms, the discotheque
against orders, martyred hoods on a headchopper road

air-strikes the headache, mortadella
the mystery, revolutionaries dizzy

baring bellies in the tightness of our love
all we wanted was bursting

such slight crimes we will die for
the line-dance with some touching

heat-seeking calm, we
got not what we came for

polite request that you spit
in my mouth before hurting

before leaving me spoiling
contraband ketchup entangled

in censorious moustache
of warm violent friend

apo apo we were talking about apo

as orphan soldiers jonesed off cigs
& continued knowing how to fix the gear
they have long known how to fix
& continued to sport tattoos of slogans
they do not know how to read

my father's work was: *peasant*
my mother's work was: *just house*

as two dogs fucked in the Raqqa road
not knowing the time had come
for going on hind legs
& afterwards, on all fours sprawled
as we kept on changing channels
in pursuit of scenes of violence
& mostly found scenes of violence
& watched *Garfield* otherwise

my date of birth is: *I don't know*
i got these scars from: *I don't know*

as we sprawled on our backs in
a boat at the riverine border
watching armed factions bloom
from cracks in the moonlight

& we told them apart
by the cries of their young

this land is: *our land*
our promise is: *revenge*

new rules

for heval R.

with 6-12 months' supply of instant noodles,
we can mount any assault upon the moon.

the floor is phosphorous. memory asphyxiates. fuck
who we were 30 seconds ago, strapping up the test
subject

without knowing the gauge of the needle or what
the wind, heavy with grit, could do to a burner,

out here under trucks, striking smokes off
the caracals, trying to think of something exciting

to make from tomorrow's inevitable beans.
Preacher, shehid, skinhead. sure. so long

as you remain horribly, perfectly sure.
under the paving-slabs, the real stone begins.

let us commit gross strategic errors, tear off
the haemostatic bandage half-healed,

tell ourselves every pose has a purpose,
knowing full well it does not. dumb as rocks,
we assume we are lice on the thigh of the war-god.
it's in the assumption we become great. comrade,

i criticise you because you never
Send me any good tunes anymore.

otherwise, we're absolved by the only good deed
that remains: being young in this old, old world.

it has been demonstrated that we, scarcely holding
onto the earth, are the only ones who will not let it
sink.

Can Yoldashim

For heval H.

distracting ourselves with intramuscular shots
on a balcony overlooking the collision
of worlds (the peeling-away of the old
from the new), over the linoleum
and into the gulf (jewel-laden chasm, peopled
with planets), so skeletally strung-out,
buzz-cut down to the skull (beyond),
blood type biro-inked in the ashy-blonde
veteran's breast (not of this war, not of this world)
not guilty not guilty, rickshaw road-trains traverse
the dazzling midnight boom-town, miraculous
six civil wars spun out on the forearm
(this ordinary sofa, this ordinary high)
peppers curl on the stove and the ashy blonde
handles the weapon (not a near-death
experience if shot in the head by a stray)
(better martyred than neck polluting the noose)
the old world flown away, the next yet to form
(not collapsed yet), pepper smoke in the embers,
shot in the thigh, rubber-limbed, sprawling,
my shooter my shooter we are not collapsed yet.

to kill the man inside

for heval T.

killdozers at the border
tube-launched, optically
tracked, wire-guided,
are all that keeps us close
both knowing the Kornet
by its smoketrail, both quite
willing to lie down hard
on separate mattresses
fisted maybe smoked-out
for sure in pigeonshit halls
six burners bursting
sleepless in each hand
readier for war with each
war that does not come

not resting well without
five bombers fanning
down the plain to keep
us close and scheming
me i'm young, dumb
still pigeon-chested
fluffed up and shrieking
dreaming of the bad-boy

jeans, the beans and eggs
you so clear-eyed
over such ugly shit
for me, love is the cheapness
vast forms in the asshole
turned on sparse evenings

for you, it's the summit
both born of the hideous
need to be noted
what it is to be kids
sculpted of vomit
by the unbearable strain
on the load-bearing living
it's not the law, clearly,
keeps us far from
such loving, it's how
we each pretend not to know
the other's true name
kept only for sharing
when the drone-strike
inevitable, yes

I wikipediaed
your saint's day
to know it
but we all have

our failures,
me so unsuited
for the world of
material objects
you so in place
so absolutely in time
yani
had we been less
than spectacular
firstly, we would not now
so gladly be grey

WhatsApp is the weapon

30,000 leaps through unencrypted channels
very unwise, fucked-up and not mandated
a boy is sent to stand on the concrete wall
which makes small boys look tall, voice thrown
squawking through the voice-note as if to say
look earth of my earth I can kill for you soon,

WhatsApp is my weapon, honey-coloured gulfs
archipelagate the filtered space where you
can't talk of kimliks or in compound verbs
can swap boot emojis for actual boots, can
project soft power over the regime-held corridor
where taxed trucks stall on frozen fronts, can say

*look far from you, far, there are spices smuggled
still to those that really fucking need them*, not
to claim the truth is worth the telephoto lens
colonoscopy, but the gun-talk of the great-aunts /
gifs of old guerrillas / prayer-bead curses of
teen mothers must be livestreamed to the weary

watched certainly by spooks but what should they
make of our loving, constellate the dark beyond
the message icon glare, the people want to talk so let
them talk in open channels, from group chat to

committee

to the world outside the camps, when the guards died
suddenly of nothing then i marked the message read ✓✓

apobaterion

for Heval B.

ugly dancing, as seems necessary to us,
leavening our hearts. white rum licks the eyeball,
leaves the socket bruised.

the dogmatists would have us court-martialled for this,
far over the oil-line, in frozen conflict.
we cannot come into one another.

when close enough to feel the pilot flame,
we're already deep in the tar. these margins
are terribly slender, yes. must they then be closed to love?

there are those who feel living well is not enough,
the guerrilla with umbrellas swerving drones on Cudi Mountain,
of course, but also those who chose to be swept along,

the people standing on their feet.
a private death is a right none of us desire,
can only feel to have been taken by force.

who can chap fingers washing dishes in the dark?
this is the real test. who can self-immolate by single degrees?

there are those made august by their crimes,
and then there are those who stumble
and keep on stumbling from the earth.
to be imperfect before the martyrs is cause for shame.

free

only in certain ways, escaping
the more obvious hells.
it is not accurate to say we have been well.

in fieri

that's militia we say, wearing it a garland of torches
tied in foxtails doing wickedness on burghers, that's
gangland in starry cities on the plain, so very harder
than your pot-plant fantasies of cycle-lanes bothered
over
put dots on all your dozers but the people are the real
prize
if the car-jackers don't get you the mothers will, furious
before it was house-to-house, not knowing your
neighbour
now we say *homeland* wearing it bloodily, crowned

everybody oil-burned under the collar yet they keep
the clothes correct, no holes in the socks, high
on handfuls of olives turning over building sites easy
women's army raised out the badlands and you
can't bring ten goons to a trash fire on May Day, still
expect to see 10x10 *chete* corpsed on the frontline
without getting the shakes (that's social drunks for you
always thronging wherever the bodies are thickest)

but it's not about that, it's dust skirl in the eighth hour
when the knee quakes laden, no we never forgot how
to do work in trench coats, that's why the standard split
the sky canary-yellow in Raqqa city, because Apo is the

family

you do not have any reckoning of, we're out here

building women's houses out of tank scraps steadily

death to Ahrar al-Sharqiya, death to all the other death boys

went masked across the border we're not masked up anymore

lifestyle treacherous

crimes for which
there is no slang

the nameless gripped
bin-liner black

we want to ride
on ararat

switch epaulettes
in cattle trucks

same body-bags
as unthanked grunts

same chickens lap
conscripted blood

but baby, baby
it's the dirty

dot x l s
the Disneyfied

the shady shit
unfetishized

o Bayraktar
come bless the brow

come test the kid
come press-gang god

come scrub the earth
of reference points

come try us now
the pin-point grief

from flight to weight
on hidden streets

cruise missile cruise
come burst our crates

the hardened hardware
shake hands shake

we have remanded
years to waste

to get our shocking
loss of faith

earth mother god
far off the face

the pincer raid
to choke the moon

the arak spilled
in silenced rooms

same chicken shit
blood type: unknown

the big one coming
soon come soon

'shame is a revolutionary virtue'

shame on the mothers
of the sons still living
shame on the party
which doesn't send them to die

shame on the upright man
in the age of downward scrabbling
shame on the non-smoker
in the age of visa-free death

shame on everything
which is anything less than everything
shame on the beast of burden
which doesn't know there is a war

shame on the poses
struck in borrowed combat trousers
shame on the other poses
struck late at night and not at will

shame on the muscle daddies
exchanging glances over me
saying *boy don't talk so much*
you were sexier when your head was shaved

internationalism

some claim subcontinental shelf & some proliferate small arms

some get stomped, some sanctioned, some are special-ops canaries

some are sports-jacket spectral with the snub-nosed in the man-bag

some are just jihadi ringos dying in the dirt

some get greasy, some get pearly, some get lit up on the mazot

some switch it up to six on shoggoth roads & drain the derricks

some spin the bottle on old stalin and shake NATO without speaking

some keep the peace by keeping garbage trucks aflame

some buck the klash & swoon & wake up in stolen country

so lost in skyline poses they forget the waste disposal sub-committee

somehow everyone is running from— and everyone is running to—

& some of you just really really really need to chill

to not self-educate is to betray

it is less important to try than to succeed.
Lenin taught us that. though perhaps we disagree,
we have found no better teacher since,
and so the lesson remains, splinter-inked among
the curter sayings of the Maoists:
le gaspillage c'est contre-révolutionnaire.

in this time of horrid rhetoric, it is necessary
we speak in primary-coloured shapes.
we listened to Lenin and, like Lenin, we speak:
if the Arab League gave no hand to Palestine,
what makes you think they will give it to you?
there, kids with stones quake tanks. like you, they are alone.

sometimes, the algorithm reveals
how little of us is known. i have sought no wife in Gaza,
nor do the villagers give a fuck about the Fertile Crescent
or the theft of fire from the woman,
wheat heads ashen, smartphone cruising,
spitting husked seeds from split lips.

sometimes, I have been rocked on blistered heels
by the tennis-shoes in which the guerrilla won

mountains,
left in filthy piles outside the bunker,
their indistinguishability indicating our companionship.
sometimes, the least earthen image
is enough to set the heart aflame.

as for the prevalence of spies,
we have come to consider it a function
and bellwether of our fame,
skipping wickedly over the earth,
craving always to take on weight.
if we become a tricontinental federation,
i don't know what we will do.
i suspect we will certainly sink.

situations

seven leagues offshore in drowning boots
still man-trapped, never did kill that informer
god damn your lamentable tea-cup poems

vegan ice-cream eaten in the most appalling fashion
all the little peshmergas really keep on running
Mummy's Revenge, al-Arabiya, back-to-back

manhood the psychosis, got to shed it to see it,
butchered up quick now the flesh twitch horrible
bless stray dogs who caught quick boots and all

the other martyrs whose flesh we write with
what we can't say, struggle session sloganeering,
screaming *biji serok apo* till the Yanks

give us over to the gunships, probably. here,
we give meaning to twenty kilos of fried chicken
piss up sniper alleys going sideways and die easy.

how you going to ban the party & complain about
the leader-cult? don't you know that gun butts
turn roaches to chrysanthemum parades

mirov wek toz e, ama hem toz hem ji xuda
who has the right to cast the stone? the one without
the F-16, obviously, still if it's on the DsHKa

you're going to know about it, yip and tang
through the cheek, out the ear, don't know about
the end times, can eat stuffed vegetables in the
interregnum

still we're really out here, still death-camp
honest when it gets to drinking, got to be
in it to taste it, got to be tire-fires for hills,

pile weight on your words when you talk
about guerilla, do not lay any more dirt on the name
of the shooters who keep chrysanthemums alive

such flags

Arin Mirkan is immortal
lighting up the death star

setting on ten centuries
like the monasteries aflame

the brave little sternums all become
shields to tanks and heavy guns

baby we are young, violent
intelligent and organised

i suppose we will get ours, some irradiated Tuesday
barrel-bomb blistered in a Captagon blaze

to survive requires more bones than we can muster
not ground-to-air missiles, not the brushing of teeth

but rather crisp autumn suicides
in wash-rooms in old England, rather

shepherd kids self-immolating
up on the karst

Google Maps sing me the distance
from the front-line to:

Temporary Northern Syria Buffer Zone, 2019-2019

the war is off again
it feels stupid to have made out wills

even steamed-out in the hospital arms-dump
begging tourniquets from the brave

wish we'd burned less irreplaceable journals
compromised OPSEC in less heartfelt ways|

now is the time for composing two sonnets
one concerning compost, the other pdfs of compost bins

not the time, this time
for the ammonium nitrate/fuel oil bombs

Stalin said: the gun and the gun
but these days there is *Kurd Idol* instead

lentils and
lentils instead

strategy of tension, slack with the years
we cannot war-plane boogie all the time

better off running the Beirut half-marathon
to raise money for indigent cats

Qamishlo

1

half the city in the kill-zone
as the grandmothers arise

bad whiskey smooths out partisans
smooth as a Syntholled arm

knight-stepping through the checkpoints
in the zone of hatched control

such spoils we have not seized
the chance for touching on the front-line

with paracetamol abusers
who know exactly how to die

those who leave in oil-tanker bellies
return in cardboard coffins

2

the airport: theirs
the border crossing: theirs

the souq: ours and theirs
the Christian quarter: theirs and ours

the militia called *Sutoro*: ours
the militia called *Sootoro*: theirs

the *shabiha*: sweet as Pepsi
the nightingale: an informer

this night: a stinking trash-fire
my nerves: cracked as eggs

the people: gathered at the roundabout
the plan: bring down unmanned drones with moon-songs

the arms: three million catapults
three million catapults: not enough

what is needed: one good Man-Portable Air Defence System
one good Man-Portable Air Defence System: not to be found

one good night's sleep: impossible
the last road east: about to fall

3

it must be all the time or let it be not at all,
the census-roll so chequered with black kisses
gutting out the names of those exempted from the war

—by which we mean the keeping-out of frogs
from well-swept keeps with snub-nosed brooms,
the leaping wildfires pissed on by the people and
the frequent loss of life for bullshit, dumb,

the sound-bomb turned too often in the palm
in the terror-zone where diplomats tread lightly,
fearing tan sands where much blood was, can be—

eroding old manners of sisters and brothers
needling ash and milk in fire-scorning brows of mothers
in the kill-box forming patties on the finger-tips, so
steady

we light up the way with smartphones,
in the martyrs' cemetery seeking out a fight we cannot handle,
Deir-ez-Zor, that's Texas, they tell you and they cackle,

Europe less a mystery with each screen-shotted shish kebab,
each foreign legion hoodlum struggling through the

lunar surf
from hood ornament *ghanima* to the trappings of a state

4

the poet and patriot Cegerxwin
is buried in Qamishlo westside
his name means *bleeding liver*
because the liver was thought
to be the seat of the humours
which is why the grandmothers say:
you are my liver
which means: you are my darling
which means: we dwell
not in the simple thump of blood
on the arterial road to the coast
but in meat rich with the fat
of five hundred molecular functions
which means, as Cegerxwin said:

if we cannot become one
we will be lost, one by one

5

replace UNSC Resolution 2254 with
flesh patties torn from each mother's

breast at the broke bell's ringing
with six-milli rounds in the Euphrates basin
in raw delight at the reasonableness
of ordinances invented by the people
with reference to the earth-mother-goddess

not here, the Geneva Process
but toddler dogfights in the foothills
of great grey mountains of gay sorrow
shrieking blissful sigh at supper-time

here where everything is crescented
and light-beams shuffle shifty
in direct glare of kings, where
it takes twelve muscles to smile
and only one to touch the trigger
and whole towns to save the barley
from garlanded IEDs

6

the kurdish zone is almost entirely our zone and the arab zone is mostly the regime's zone but there are so many arabs in the kurdish zone now it doesn't really make sense to call it the kurdish zone anymore. the assyrian zone and the syriac zone are the same zone and mostly contiguous with the armenian zone, though these should on no account be confused. parts of the syriac-assyrian-armenian zones are in our zone and parts are in the regime zone and you can't go into the regime zone except for when you can, which is sometimes, and where you can, which is in some places. the regime zone has the best cheeseburgers but you might get disappeared or electrocuted for going there. our zone has less of both cheeseburgers and electrocutions. nonetheless aeroplanes, UN staff and WHO donations arrive only into the regime zone because the regime zone is a real zone and our zone does not exist except in the experience of several million people. the UN and the WHO agree with the regime that there is nothing to be done about this. there was a sort of NGO zone in our zone but they all ran away during the war and they mostly haven't come back. all of the aforementioned zones are also in the russian zone and also in the american zone and sort of in neither, depending on who you ask, but let's not get into that now. don't even get me started on iran. all of these zones are also in the official international safe zone which means literally nothing. in the sky there is a deconfliction zone but that's for russia and america and turkey and a little bit for the regime and not for us. we are definitely not allowed even a millimetre of zone in the sky.

along the zones of hatched control in the souq and at the fringes of our zone and the regime zone and along the street which is called *al-Corniche* though it is a waterfront to nothing, only a dribble of sewage and piss and dust, the city is breaking apart. *yani*: the city is becoming a smashed-up chequerboard of zones, zones forming under the weight of zones, not just the kurdish zone and the arabic zone and the russian zone and the american zone and the assyrian-syriac-armenian zone and the regime zone and our zone but also the street-corner zone and the commune zone and the refugee zone and the cooperative zone and the old-women-on-patrol zone and the gossiping-old-men zone and the home zone, all of them so smashed up you can't tell which zone is which any more, which, though this is not how we planned it, is what we hoped for all along.

7

your piss is sweeter than all the sherbets of those tyrants —
Cegerxwin

8

Maoist salmon surfed
midnight villages in silence

spread the word
without their shoes on

left messages for one another
in children's thirsty mouths

now they come into the city
shelter in the cross-hatched zone

eat ketchup pizza and are grateful
for drones pattering like rain

when tomorrow the city falls
they will melt into the wheat-field west

each one has her mountain
she will bring her mountain with her

she will fertilise it
with the teeth of the dead

9

when asked by hacks
where are the people?
i grin so shitty starry

they are here in every gesture
raising dust from boom-box floorboards
bleeding stemmed with bootleg filters

scrabbling for a lighter
in the pockets of resistance
welling up in public meetings

it must be everything but
everything can be hot-wired
the price of losing pace

must be the high-wire execution
the cut-short fall and dangle
between zones that won't stop drifting

you say

Assad or we burn the country

we

are nothing if not burning

booster rockets in Jazira
pouring flames down al-Corniche

Qamishlo is NES' largest Kurdish-majority city and de facto capital. It is also home to sizeable Armenian and Syriac-Assyrian Christian minorities who founded the city, as well as a major Arab population. Most of the city is controlled by the Autonomous Administration of North and East Syria, but some neighbourhoods and thoroughfares, plus the airport and border crossing with Turkey, remain controlled by the Assad regime.

III – Operation Peace Spring

balance sheet

The situation is:

more war in the safe zone
than out of it

300,000 fled
from the secure zone for IDPs

six years of digging tunnels
still we can't keep
our heads above the earth

the people pelt
the Americans with stones
not wanting them to leave

the situation is:

we have to hope the F-16s will strike
the front-lines tonight
to prove the ceasefire has failed

a drone strike does not count
as an air strike, they say:

those torn apart may feel otherwise
but they are hardly an independent source

we all want our own drone strike
but there aren't enough to go round

someone has to do the dishes
someone has to keep account
someone has to pay back

the oxygen debt
the sleep debt
the blood debt

someone has to answer
for all the times we foolishly
felt free on the checkpointed roads

for our enemies

we hate how we're made to beg for it all
what we scrabble after
what we thirst for as it spills

we hate how dear friends have unbuckled themselves
how centripetal the weight
of the times we have failed

we hate the way we kiss on both cheeks
to check how much meat
remains on the bone

and how grateful we are

for the extra hour snatched
below blankets in the safehouse
the beans slow to come to the boil

for our paths which, though threaded
through black gaps between checkpoints,
nonetheless contrive to coincide

for the drone which pins us down
in this culvert together
heat-seeking the burning of our thighs

despite all pressures to the contrary, then,
we have nonetheless contrived to be alive

ISIS withdraw from their last urban stronghold, Hajin, Deir-ez-Zor

how evident it is who has known pain precisely once, who is at ease adjacent to the killing fields,

tending toward the light at its most terribly bright. journalists, not touching their tea,

demand images of reed-spined men. *is that the reediest you have?* they ask.

meanwhile, in the reed-beds, the situation is very bad. women, uncaged, run toward women,

men vault the crocus bloom of dead men's fingers. the heart, bicameral, ugly,

is galvanised by reconstituted chicken meat, the noodles rehydrated by the burning rain.

though the jasmine folds sooner than communicate chlorophyll to its companions,

this does not prove it has never known heat; only that, for now, each petal holds in reserve

what it has known of harvesting machines, the drain-sweet tang of pesticides, the stench of beards

shaved off and cast into the oil-drum where the militiawomen keep counsel, for example,

knowing themselves an example, knowing the use of the Kalashnikov in suppressing return fire,

and other gambits they rightly should not. to take succour from such severe degrees is possible, yes.

here among us, under the processing blade, are many who now count one another as neighbours,

the frock-coated freak wasting munitions on fowl, for example, the conscripts in shambles,

those who caught their breath and will not let it go; all strike the same salted well in their thirst.

a particular film coats the teeth, the tongue. in time, wire wool will scour flesh to the bone, beyond,

the pint glass will knock against the nerve. already plaster snowflakes, induced by distant mortars;

soon, the Hellfire will come knocking on our roof. soon, we must describe it well.

the risk is that war will not unfold, the shock go unshared between shoulders in basements,

that each will bend in his or her own way. we must call upon the people more and more.

the risk is that we will end up quaking in separate kebab joints, the last chance for a brokered peace

lost as we speak dispassionately of the merits of heavy weapons, that we are out here

and will linger past the twisted lips of the harbour, boiling on the hot-wired hob, the heat

which denatured the fundamental protein become a necessary condition of existence.

absence of evidence

berms held long enough
that the townsfolk can flee
not having packed up their possessions
not having believed in war

the heaviest shelling ended
on the thirteenth
rather than the fourteenth
of the month

or so we have to hope
there is no proof

we could only make the world
believe in war
after the fact
after the war

a handful kept alive
for a handful of days
on the jury-rigged iron lung

how many would have choked
otherwise? we do not know

there is no justification
for any single stroke

it is only the lessening
of slaughter
through slaughter
which has been

empirically

proved

for Hevrin Khalef

the temptation is to elide
normalise or over-indulge
and not to inhabit

but this is our work
to dwell in the wound
of the occipital pit

not only to trace gravel in flesh
flight of the fighters
kick-back and bruise

but to reconstitute
from post-mortem proofs
a life riding Huawei

speaker-phone with an aunt
whose well has drawn dust
these eight years of the smoke

to remake the meat
of the leaky stove sit-down
in unfriendly times

to people the portraits
flash-bulb-caught in their prime
with bellies and pamphlets

of shrewd recommendations
and twinklings of grief

for the young are so ready

to haemorrhage freely
to become uninhabited
lighter than smoke

the truth is not
the sum of abrasions
but the abrasions
attest to the truth

Hevrin Khalef was a leading female Syrian Kurdish politician. During the 2019 invasion, she was dragged from her car, beaten and shot dead by militiamen controlled by the occupying Turkish forces.

when elephants dance

we dance the last dabke for the camera-phones' sake:
the beat will keep our threat alive for those who come after,
picking up the scent from the city dump, understanding
black flags once burned here, where black flags now fly.

don't you believe paving slabs can leap to conscripted hands?
you will. all forgot razorblades could be sewn in the velvet cap,
all save she who wore it, one eye glittering at the press,
sugar on the finger-tips to keep the blood up for the kill.

do you know how long a hate-filled soul can run
on half a salted onion and ten packs of cigarettes?
there exist lips which smack at poison, dehydration;
I could go on. they will speak to you in time.

each morning friends of ours pace prison-yard circuits
in certain meadows. do you understand that certain postures
are scorched in flesh? that some muscles do not cramp
but grow stronger when the stress position is enforced?

you're thirsty to uncover the absolute limit, the questions
to which answers spring unbidden in the throat.
the thought this limit lies outside your black sites
is wicked to you, isn't it? doesn't it make you feel sick?

you studied them and thought they didn't study you
because they wrote no books; did it not occur
that languages, once banned, would
reach a pitch inaudible to your ears?

do you really want to boogie? do you really
trust your hit-men? do you understand what we mean
when we claim to be present in the scent
of the smoke rising from the bombed-out dancehall?

do not come closer. you may shout your answers from there.

for M., in England

we busy ourselves with death for
nineteen and a half hours daily
afterward, for sixteen
afterward, for twelve

with a break, in the afternoon,
for lying face-down waiting
for the wi-fi to restart; and
I begin to think of thinking about

writing home to you, who never
shamed me for not writing
even when the bombs were falling
for nineteen hours a day

who never tried to ask
a thing about the war, and so
understood it better than most

to the retreating convoy

tell it to the mothers stirring great big pots of beans
to feed the solid-bellied women in the killing machine

smoking cigarettes that really smoke
tar kick-drum thump the lung

some bedbugs in the creases
of syriacivilwarmap dot com

flat-headed scarlet unsquashables
running from the butcher thumb:

how your risk analysts always open
their fucking awful gargoyle mouths

saying: *should* and *shouldn't have*
saying: *might have been saved*

like this was ever about strategy
about anything but flames

Peace Spring

many small crimes will be swallowed up.
the odds against the back-hoe-loader execution are great.

as such, we must surrender small arms into the grasp
of those who have wished us concrete harm.

we must adjust our own, in the seat
of oversized pants, as easily as settling an itch.

we must accept itches and the likelihood of voice-notes left
unanswered, in the context of forcible demographic change.

what occasion to learn the unblinking acceptance
of black-out naps and the reheated rice dishes of neighbours,

guessing at geopolitics round a substitute hearth.
we must attain the annual conference at all costs.

there are those who must do quite terrible things, the lacing
Of landmines though tuk-tuks, the falsification of customs declarations.

we don't have to commit more wrong than we can bear,
though we must be prepared to account for those who do.
nor do we need to bulk up our frame with three pullovers
for the short run to the barbershop, but we do it anyway,

to feel a part of what we are a part of.
there are worse crimes than wanting to be real.

there are indications everything is going very badly.
(we must kneel and blow on the embers of lost lives.)

perhaps they still aren't going badly enough.
perhaps we must return to the days of the grain.

we must do all this and yet remain clear,
when struck, like a bell.

IV – marvellous as fancy parakeets

ceasefire

people want very much to lay out six packets
of crisps and three tins of tomato paste
on a trestle-table outside their bombed-out house.
they will die for this, laying hands

on unexploded mines. but then they will die
if it is not done, the heart sometimes just stopping:
or else they self-immolate, six years later,
in front of the UNICEF offices.

human rights are over-large, hygienic,
armour-plated with guarantees: almost all
will waive them gladly for the two-foot garden
and the shrubs grown in old tomato tins.

people want very much to hang up
bright pink pairs of socks between walls
smeared with ash and sometimes blood,
to offer the second-to-last cigarette

from a crushed-up packet to a neighbour
not blamed for the sins of his sons.
and if there are eight families living
in one abandoned petrochemical plant,

for sure they will divide the turbine-hall
with curtains and respect one another's space.
perhaps they will organise themselves
via a committee of sorts, share out the cooking-oil,

teach the children to read and write in a minor
mother-tongue, do their laundry via rota,
let their two-foot gardens flow into
one long melon patch. i only say perhaps.

it is not cost-effective to be cruel.

Peace Spring ii

for Sarah

six people in the world i can meet
for a pint without having a pint before

half of them half the world away
o the intercontinental dark

half of them not long for living
o the intercontinental dark

indelible the stains, the stamps
the visa denied by a bloody palm

the mortgaging of tomorrow's home to come home to
for the vanished night in the maoist stockade

terrified to cross, not the final inch, but
the frontex frontline and the offshore flames

with schedule #7 of the terror act (2000)
with the courage no-one asked us to have

they keep us from us
were we wrong to be brave

International volunteers returning from NES to Western countries face repression, imprisonment, and state harassment in some cases leading to suicide. Upon my return, I was briefly imprisoned in a number of migrant detention centres in Europe and—along with other UK volunteers—banned from the 27 states of the Schengen Zone for 10 years.

-

pathogen unknown
in solidarity with the Stansted 15

disease X represents

flash-drives full of martyred friends
murals whose eyes you can't gouge out
secret slide-shows shown on bedsheets
to guerrilla hiding in the hills

out to straight lawyers who do good regardless
of the dumb shit we told you contingent at stansted
intestines aclank with vaselined data
swearing blind all thirteen ugly lovers
paraded onscreen are unknown

out to lesbian mothers, card-scammers, scumbag paramedics
the class coalescing for want of a class

we breathe on you breathe on you breathe

willingly, we foreclose all futures not
ending in grief, slide back the paper
unsigned. pathogenic plexiglass huff:
moue: a banned word traced in the filth

you are all called 'call me': 'call me nichola', 'call me john'
call me craig says: 'we just don't understand *why*.
why, being from a good home like yours, would one
consciously accept the status of a bomb?'

i denounce all craigs and proffered meal deals
i exorcise the cop you put in our heads
i will not mourn those who, explicitly seeking life,
died only in the most trivial sense

i mourn only her banned hand on mine in the pocket
of the concrete overcoat, more blanketed
by maggi powder than the stars. i conceal only
his saying: *you know how to sell smoke*

his erection obvious and hidden
on the back of the dirt-bike
running memory cards through
the demilitarised zone

NATO was myth
fit for infants and scholars

Schengen was smoke
now cops count my teeth

the way they ask: *why*
is itself cause enough
craig

i confess
i self-indict
i reveal

i trust

in reckless proclamations of love through the encrypted app
sweet enough to radicalise the judge

in the incendiary touch of hands between friends
that brings down the plane from the sky

for Anna Campbell (Helin Qerechox)

we would
but we will not
because we cannot do that

after that we would
we would not rest until we had
but our enemies are
so we cannot do that either

above all, we would also
in our thousands we would also
believe us, *heval*
at any cost we would also

but your body is not
we cannot even do that

you said: if you love your own
enough to fight for and to die for
(and you must love your own
enough to fight for and to die for)
you have to love the far from
enough to fight for and to die for

your saying weighs upon
every day it weighs upon
we cannot enough
we cannot enough

we can only this and that
in little towns here and there
which hug the border though it burns
which you fought for and died for
and made chai for and were for
we can only house by house
woman by woman we can

until we die for
until we cannot
until we die for
or
until

Anna Campbell was a British woman who lost her life fighting to defend Afrin during Turkey's 2018 invasion and occupation.

Korinthos pre-removal detention centre

you must risk it all,
once or twice.
i cannot tell you where or when.

this does not mean the time and place
are unimportant: rather,
you will know them when you see them.

you must not get into fights without your boots on.
you must not die with your socks on.
whether you lunge or not is up to you.

no matter how long the night, how hard the bunk,
how loud the na'at from the Bluetooth speaker in the next cell,
you must never ask your neighbour to turn it down.

in old age, you will come
to envy yourself
these awful, sleepless nights.

reduction

almost naked, but not quite:
i have my shorts, my cardboard fan,

my bit of wood for cleaning under the nails:
i had better hold on to these.

if the boy in the next bunk hangs himself,
as the betting is he will, a queue

will form for his bed-sheet. torn up
it would do for a belt, if not a noose,

although another boy hung himself in the toilet
with a phone-charger, not two months ago.

(the quality of the workmanship
continues to amaze.)

i have my Norwegian paperback for a table,
my plastic fork for a comb.

we have our cardboard chute
for sliding treats between cells:

sugar, sleeping pills, half a travel brochure
with beautiful girls inside.

today the heavens broke and it roared
with rain and the boys ran out into the yard,

naked, screaming with laughter,
and shampooed their hair.

but i didn't join them: i had three cigarettes:
i didn't want to lose them, nor get them wet.

prison sestina iv

cell 1 slides cell 3 a crumpled-up napkin
concealing the last crumb of hashish.
cell 3 checks both sides for a message,
but cell 1 exchanged their last biro
for a time-share in the blackjack-stamped lighter.
best to smoke out the crooked days inside.

desperate to turn out their insides
some scrawl maledictions on brown paper napkins
speak smoke words in circles of hashish
condemn the employer who left their message
on read, battery drained as the biro
spent against beton: *weighed, measured, found lighter*.

if the guys do split lips for the lighter
they may seem skulled on the fumes, but inside
they fold demon birds out of napkins
take off for Saturn, ringed by the hashish,
each knowing only he sees the message
hid in the quadrille spoon-towel-razor-biro.

as Khaled melts down the biro
to pierce the mattress so it's lighter
to dead-lift once emptied of its insides,
so prison drains a man of stashed napkins,
lightens his heart with time, talk and hashish.
and if the question is courage, the message

of who will endure is transparently messaged
on brows, like the sentence tattooed, biro-
ink in the breast, with needle and lighter

we remind ourselves that we are inside
walls that won't be unmade, no napkins
to tear, nothing melts into air, hashish

is only hashish and when the hashish
smoke clears it leaves us no message:
pause. i exhale and reach for the biro.
though the day be no shorter, the night no lighter
and the sky remains to define what is inside,
still, I feel the need to record on my napkins

how the napkins unfurl round this absence of hashish
this unanswered message, drained biro, spent lighter,
this empty cell holding everything inside.

david wojnarowicz drinks a tea in kobane

queer, isn't it?

the noting down of names
in a little black book
to be remembered
or at least once written down
we have wanted very badly to be well

to secretly always hope to lose
to day-dream deaths as marvellous
as fancy parakeets
to know things not taught
like how to cum when you are hungry
so the hunger goes away
for a while
there is some satiety in it

queer, how you can tell the old
from the young by the weight of their hands
those not yet maimed
you can tell by their hands
they have wanted very badly to be well

but now we have no friends left
save our crimes, we know

that five a day is a fatality
the thing is to be sick
to pour and keep on pouring
to be vectors of disease

no seatbelts no seatbelts no seatbelts no seatbelts

an unmarked taxi is the least of my fears

through the bars

the boy peels an orange in a third-floor window.
the guard below shouts him to stop.
the boy sheds scraps of peel.

the breeze is cool.
the guard fails to benefit from it,
perspiring on the asphalt track.

the boy drinks the oceanic pole of inaccessibility.
the breeze can't wash juice from sticky fingers,
nor change what can't be changed.

the boy spits a pip.
who was it claimed Persephone
preferred the sunlit world?

the guard will come up there,
kick the shit out the boy,
just you wait and see.

the boy smiles serenely, knowing he is
up three flights of stairs & behind six steel doors
at the state's behest, is, therefore, quite safe.

the seasons turn,
give up their tribute
of six small rubies.

the shades—though no-one thought
to seek their opinion on this—
consider themselves ransomed enough.

mucky pups

in each war zone there are several shiftless dogs
responsible for supping the blood of the dead.
don't hasten to judge those who have grown
a taste for what others weren't asked to lick.
some have littler fleas, some were flea-bit
from the start. Blake was cannibalized
by a man-sized ghost. others are born with
the terrible itch that won't be scratched,
only bled. meet me at the Square of the
Martyrs of the Previous War but One. i will
be wearing my dirtiest skin. you will
channel babushka vibes, by which I mean
you will love that which you love very hard.
how the brown Humber gives up rubies.
how a greasy strand can be a nation, the seat
of more endurance than can be endured.
we will circle one another in a sunlit plaza,
each sniffing (metaphorically) the other's arse.
we will know one another again. and more.

these are the years

"Remember, these are the years in which it is not a matter of winning victories but of winning the defeats…"
– Bertolt Brecht

we grew large in the revolution,
flapping out our arms, swelling to occupy
the given space. afterward very small,
very fast, rushing past hard limits with no
knee-pads on. brave face. dumb fuck.
so many ways to get boxed off quick.
some, we will find out hard.

the various youths on their various phones
have borne witness to all manner of atrocities,
and we have tasted the worst of October,
under skies so laden with munitions
it seems Vulcan must make there his mine.

we grew accustomed, very fast,
to the different varieties of death,
learning which should be feared
(only the pot-bellied funny-man unfurling
to reveal the lacerating loss of three friends),
which catch a migrating bullet
(death of death: even old Pluto craves

the short, sharp blow to the head),
and which is laughed at (almost all).

cotton-mouthed, wasp-washed,
four packs a day and rising,
blurting out absolutions
we didn't mean to extend.
this, the constant of months.

now we move neighbourhoods and assume
new rhythms of electricity availability,
a new commune, quite the same
as the old. (this continuity goes
unremarked by the New York Times.)

friends are lost, but mostly
through quick, bird-like acts of treachery,
the kind done to save twenty minutes' commute.
our calm, collected speech is
the knife prising up the epidermis,
excising the unearned tattoo.

we held our breath through the long
year of the bean. we laid no claim
save the no-fly-zone, and everyone knows
how that turned out. we, who have
known continents flip over and burn,

cannot empathise with the rules-based
international order: not yet.
we ourselves will keep on winning,
regardless of our incalculable loss.

we, who warned of the megaton extinction event,
could not ourselves be present at the blast.

say mental health awareness week
one more time, motherfucker, we are exploding
every which way save the obvious,
off the shoulders of the front-lines, in the bush-fires
breathing, too stoned to cope and
still operating the necessary killing machine,
because if we stop killing we will die.

(Chorus: we must stop killing in order to live.)

we ourselves expect no charity. how could we?
what we want, no-one has ever had before.

Acknowledgements:

Without the Rojava revolution this collection would never have come to be. Indeed, it is strange now to recall that there was a time when a contested strip of land in northern Syria was not at the centre of my life and work, and difficult to imagine how I would have survived the past few years without it.

When it comes to thanks, it is quite impossible to know where to start – with my colleagues in RIC and across NES who stood and stand together in such difficult circumstances, providing immeasurable love, support, criticism, rage, laughter and comradeship? With the Kurdish movement itself, which gave me the chance to travel to Kurdistan on the basis of a speculative email, enabled me to learn so much from what was happening there, and placed trust in us to work freely and openly to make the situation in NES known around the world? With the thousands of hevals, unknown personally to me, who spent decades working in the shadows and sacrificing all they had so that one day the revolution could burst into life?

And so I will simply say *silav u rez* to all of my comrades – both those whom I know, and who know who they are, and all those who are part of the struggle for freedom which unites us across continents and decades alike. *An serkeftin an serkeftin.*

Deep thanks to Isabelle Kenyon and the Fly on the Wall team for giving me the opportunity to bring this collection into the world, supporting me so thoroughly throughout the process – and even spotting the typo in 'hypoosmolality'. Deep thanks to my mentor Anthony Anaxagorou for his wise and precise interventions, without which the collection could never have taken shape. Deep thanks to the Arts Council, the Society of Authors, and Future's Venture for providing the financial support which allowed me to work on the book following my return to the UK.

Thanks also to the following magazines, websites and anthologies for publishing several of these poems elsewhere, sometimes in a different form:

- *road repair works continue in Tirbespi* – originally published by Rise Up Review
- *kisses rough through the skimask but* – originally published by Glass Poetry
- *safe zone* – originally published by Ink, Sweat and Tears
- *such flags* – originally published by Protean
- *Qamishlo* – originally published by Tahoma Literary Review
- *for Hevrin Khalef* – originally published by Stand
- *when elephants dance* – originally published by Agenda
- *ceasefire* – originally published by Best New British and Irish Poets 2020/2021
- *pathogen unknown* – originally published by Poets

- Reading The News
- *korinthos pre-removal detention centre* – originally published by Prole
- *reduction* – originally published by Prole
- *through the bars* – originally published by Prole

And of course, endless thanks to my family and friends in the UK and Europe for putting up with all of this; providing beds and sofas when I arrived back in the country in the middle of lockdown, unwashed and somewhat slightly dazed; supporting me during my brief sojourn in the Greek detention system; and being there when it was needed most.

Glossary

- Afrin: Kurdish-majority region of NES attacked, occupied and ethnically cleansed by Turkey and its proxy militias in 2018

- Ahrar al-Sharqiya: Turkish-controlled militia sanctioned by the USA for committing multiple war crimes against the Kurdish population and recruiting former ISIS members

- Amed prison: A 1982 hunger strike in Turkey's Amed (Diyarbakir) prison was foundational to the Kurdish freedom movement. With thousands of members, supporters and affiliates imprisoned in Turkey and across the globe, including many Kurdish MPs, the hunger strike is a tactic the movement has continued until this day, with jailed female Kurdish MP Leyla Guven leading a major hunger strike in 2018.

- Anna Campbell: British woman who lost her life in defence of Afrin during the 2018 Turkish invasion (see below)

- Arin Mirkan: Kurdish woman and YPJ commander who sacrificed her life to halt a tank assault during the 2014 battle against ISIS in Kobane (see below)

- Autonomous Administration of North and East Syria (AANES): Political body made up of regional and devolved councils, with day-to-day responsibility for administering NES

- Apo: Nickname for Öcalan (see below)

- Arak: Anise-based liquor drunk in Syria and across the region

- 'Assad or we burn the country': Slogan displayed, chanted and graffitied by Syrian regime supporters across the country

- Armenian: A primarily-Christian ethnic group also resident in NES, who have achieved new protections and freedoms as they participate autonomously in the SDF and AANES

- Assyriac-Syrian: A Christian ethnic group also resident in NES, who have achieved new protections and freedoms as they participate autonomously in the SDF and AANES

- Bayraktar: Turkish-made armed, unmanned drone named for Erdoğan's son-in-law and used to devastating effect against the Kurdish movement and in proxy conflicts across the region

- 'Berxwedan jiyan e': 'resistance is life', slogan of the Kurdish freedom movement

- Bilancho: Daily total of those killed and wounded in the war

- Captagon: Amphetamine drug widely abused by combatants in the Syrian war

- Cegerxwin: Kurdish poet, author and nationalist activist

- Commune: Neighbourhood assembly which is the lowest level of devolved political organisation in NES

- Corniche: principal street in Qamishlo, still bearing its French colonial name

- Criticism and self-criticism: Process of group

accountability and personal political development practiced by the Kurdish movement

- Cudi Mountain: mountain and PKK stronghold in Bakur (Turkish Kurdistan): a traditional site of Noah's 'apobaterion', the location where his ark came to rest, predating the identification of Mount Ararat

- Chete: derogatory Kurdish term for a member of ISIS, the Turkish-controlled proxy militias, or another radical Islamist or criminal organisation; literally 'flea', thus 'bandit'

- Dabke: Traditional Arab dance

- Deir-ez-Zor: Eastern region of NES which was the site of ISIS' last stand as a military force, and still a hotbed of ISIS sleeper-cell activity

- Democratic confederalism: System of devolved, regional or municipal direct democracy advocated for by Abdullah Öcalan, and which has found its fullest expression in NES

- Diyarbakir: Largest Kurdish city in Bakur (Turkish Kurdistan), and a centre of political resistance and PKK activity

- DShK: Heavy machine-gun widely used in Syria

- Erbil: Major city in Bashur (Iraqi Kurdistan)

- Ghanima: Arabic term meaning 'spoils of war'

- Govend: Traditional Kurdish dance

- Heval: Kurdish word for 'friend', also used to mean 'comrade'

- Hevrin Khalef: Leading female Syrian Kurdish

politician dragged from her car, beaten and shot dead by militiamen controlled by the occupying Turkish forces during the 2019 invasion

- Internationalist: Used to describe any foreign volunteer who has travelled to NES to work in solidarity with the 'Rojava revolution', in a civilian or military capacity

- Jazira: one of the principal regions of NES, home to Qamishlo and other major Kurdish and Arabic settlements

- Kobane: Kurdish city which was the site of ISIS' first major defeat, as the Kurdish YPG and YPJ managed to break out of a siege and push ISIS back. The victory won international attention

- Kornet: Russian-made anti-tank guided missile

- Kurdistan Region of Iraq: Semi-autonomous region of Kurdistan forming part of the Iraqi state

- Kurdistan Regional Government (KRG): Governs the semi-autonomous Kurdistan Region of Iraq. Dominated by the KDP, a conservative Kurdish party hostile to NES and the PKK

- Kurdistan Workers' Party (PKK): Kurdish-led militant group fighting the Turkish Government with the aim of establishing a system of federal, devolved democracy ('democratic confederalism') in Turkey and throughout the region

- Kimlik: Turkish identity card

- Klash: AK-47 or Kalashnikov rifle, ubiquitous throughout the region

- MANPADS: Man-portable Air-Defense System, a highly in-demand weapon in the region
- Mazot: Crude diesel, used for heating and as fuel oil
- Medya Defence Zones: Mountainous region of Bashur (Iraqi Kurdistan) under the de facto control of the PKK
- Na'at: South Asian poetry in praise of the Prophet Mohammed
- Nave tevgera: 'movement name', pseudonym adopted by volunteers with the Kurdish political movement
- North and East Syria (NES): Autonomous region of Syria built around the Kurdish region of 'Rojava', defended by the SDF, and administered by the AANES under the principle of 'democratic confederalism'
- Öcalan, Abdullah: Imprisoned Kurdish political leader, PKK founder, and the key theorist of the new form of political organisation known as 'democratic confederalism'
- 'Peace Spring': Turkey's official name for the 2019 military operation which saw it capture 5000KM^2 of NES territory, killing hundreds and displacing hundreds of thousands of civilians. Turkey was able to achieve its objectives of invading and ethnically cleansing a large strip of the border, but could not seize the majority of NES' territory
- Peshmerga: Armed forces controlled by the Kurdistan Regional Government, hostile to the SDF and PKK

- PKK: See 'Kurdistan Workers' Party'
- Qamishlo: Largest Kurdish-majority city and de facto capital of NES, divided into zones of NES and Assad regime control
- Raqqa: Former de facto capital of ISIS, now part of NES following its 2017 liberation by the SDF – it is the region's largest city
- Rojava: West Kurdistan, or that region of Kurdistan previously occupied by the Syrian government; these Kurdish-majority regions were the basis
- Rojava revolution: The establishment, maintenance and expansion of democratic autonomy across northern and eastern Syria following the outbreak of civil war in Syria
- Safe zone: Turkey claimed it wanted to establish a 'safe zone' all along the Turkish-Syrian border as justification for its devastating 2019 military operation against NES. Following the 'ceasefire' agreement, the border region is de facto divided between Turkish and NES control, in what is officially a new 'safe zone' patrolled by US and Russian forces but where conflict remains a daily reality
- Sakine Cansiz: A leading female figurehead of the Kurdish freedom movement, who spent years in jail in Turkey, facing torture and other abuses. She and two other female Kurdish activists were shot dead in a Kurdish Cultural Centre in Paris in 2013, by a gunman linked to the Turkish-controlled Grey Wolves fascist paramilitary group
- Schedule #7: Power under the Terror Act (2000)

enabling the UK Government to detain and question people at ports of entry to the UK, without the right to silence or refuse to hand over electronics passwords. Widely used against supporters of the Kurdish movement

- Souq: Market

- Sutoro: Assyriac-Syrian Christian armed force based in the Christian neighbourhood of Qamishlo, which works with the SDF

- Sutoroo: Assyriac-Syrian Christian armed force based in the Christian neighbourhood of Qamishlo, but loyal to Assad

- Syrian Democratic Forces (SDF): The official armed forces of NES, which worked with US backing to lead the defeat of ISIS on the ground and have also fought against the Turkish Armed Forces, their proxies, and Assad government forces

- Sere Kaniye: One of two once-ethnically diverse cities attacked, occupied and ethnically cleansed by Turkey and its proxy militias in 2019

- Shehid: Martyr, any individual who has given their life in the struggle against ISIS and Turkey to establish democratic confederalism in the region

- Shabiha: Loose militias sponsored by the Assad government (literally, 'ghost')

- Sulaymaniyah: Major city in Bashur (Iraqi Kurdistan)

- Tel Abyad: One of two once-ethnically diverse cities attacked, occupied and ethnically cleansed by Turkey and its proxy militias in 2019

- Til Temir: Multi-ethnic town on the frontlines between NES and the Turkish-occupied regions

- TLAM: Tomahawk Land Attack Missile, a USA-operated cruise missile

- Yezidi: Ancient, syncretic religion which has suffered long persecution and an attempted genocide by ISIS in 2014; Yezidis in their homeland of Shengal were rescued from genocide by the PKK, while Yezidis resident in NES have achieved new protections and freedoms as they participate autonomously in the SDF and AANES

- YPG: 'People's Defence Units', Kurdish-led Syrian armed formation which forms the backbone of the SDF

- YPJ: 'Women's Defence Units', Kurdish-led, all-female armed formation which fights alongside the YPG and is another key component of the SDF

About the Author

Matt Broomfield is a British poet, journalist and activist who spent 2018-2020 living and working in Rojava, North and East Syria, in solidarity with the Kurdish-led revolution there. While in Syria he co-founded the Rojava Information Centre, the region's top independent, English-language news source. He is now back in the UK, where he continues his writing, journalism and advocacy around Rojava and Kurdistan, among other issues.

His poetry has been published by the Tahoma Literary Review, Stand, Ink, Sweat and Tears, Agenda, Glass, the National Poetry Society, the Independent and the Best New British And Irish Poets 2021, among others; his poetry was shared across London by Poetry On The Underground; and he is a former Foyle Young Poet of the Year. *brave little sternums* is his debut full-length collection.

About Fly on the Wall Press

A publisher with a conscience.
Political, Sustainable, Ethical.
Publishing politically-engaged, international fiction, poetry and cross-genre anthologies on pressing issues. Founded in 2018 by founding editor, Isabelle Kenyon.

Some other publications:

The Woman With An Owl Tattoo by Anne Walsh Donnelly
The Prettyboys of Gangster Town by Martin Grey
The Sound of the Earth Singing to Herself by Ricky Ray
Inherent by Lucia Orellana Damacela
Medusa Retold by Sarah Wallis
Pigskin by David Hartley
We Are All Somebody
Aftereffects by Jiye Lee
Someone Is Missing Me by Tina Tamsho-Thomas
Odd as F*ck by Anne Walsh Donnelly
Muscle and Mouth by Louise Finnigan
Modern Medicine by Lucy Hurst
These Mothers of Gods by Rachel Bower
Sin Is Due To Open In A Room Above Kitty's by Morag Anderson
Fauna by David Hartley
How To Bring Him Back by Clare HM
Hassan's Zoo and A Village in Winter by Ruth Brandt
No One Has Any Intention of Building A Wall by Ruth Brandt

Social Media:

@fly_press (Twitter) @flyonthewall_poetry (Instagram)
@flyonthewallpress (Facebook) www.flyonthewallpress.co.uk